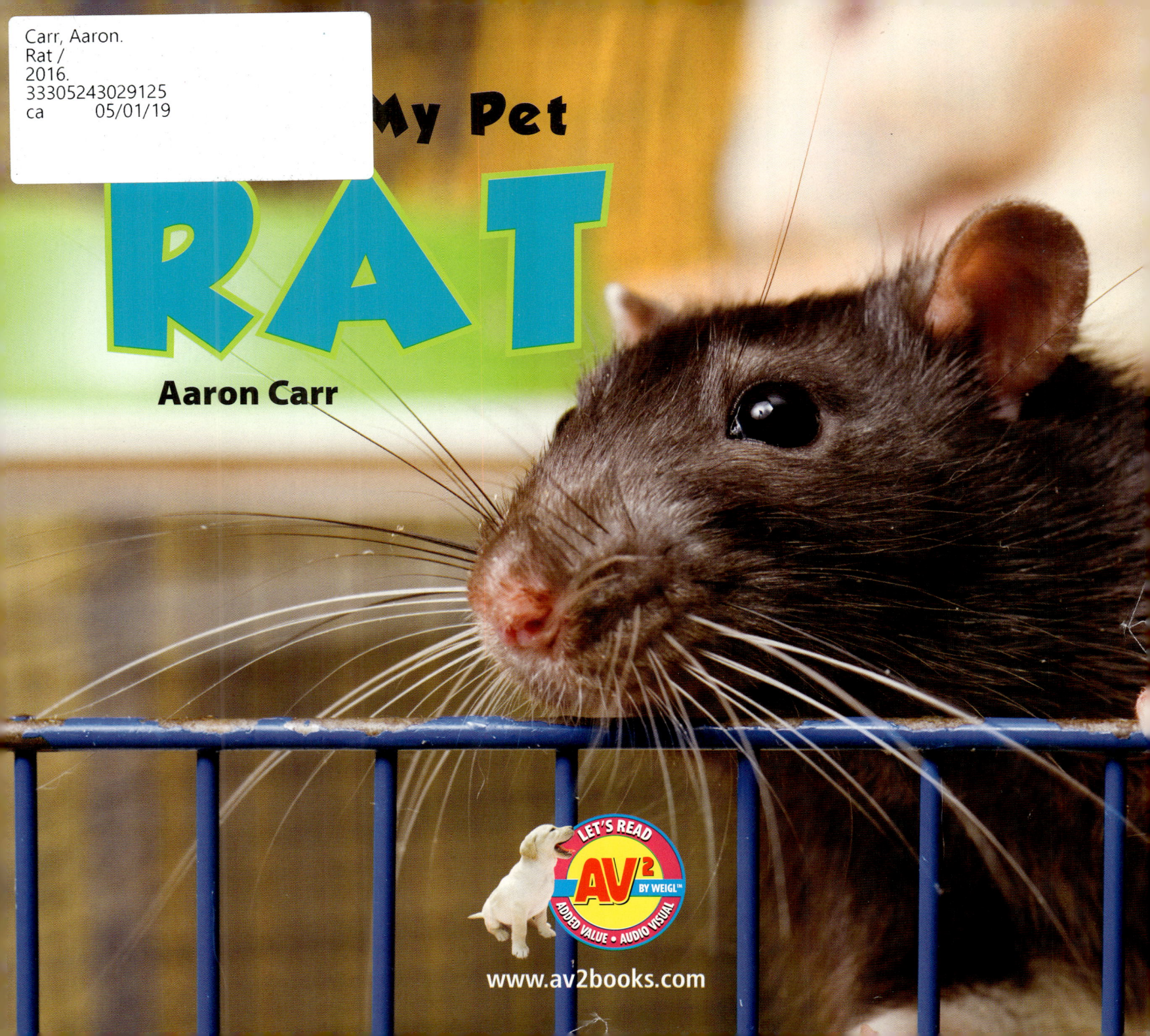

My Pet
RAT

Aaron Carr

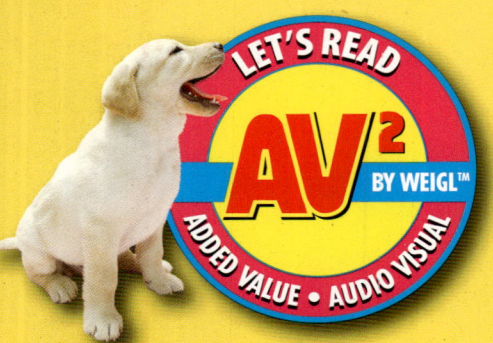

AV² provides enriched content that supplements and complements this book. Weigl's AV² books strive to create inspired learning and engage young minds in a total learning experience.

Your AV² Media Enhanced books come alive with...

 **Audio**
Listen to sections of the book read aloud.

 **Key Words**
Study vocabulary, and complete a matching word activity.

 **Video**
Watch informative video clips.

 **Quizzes**
Test your knowledge.

 **Embedded Weblinks**
Gain additional information for research.

 **Slide Show**
View images and captions, and prepare a presentation.

 **Try This!**
Complete activities and hands-on experiments.

Go to www.av2books.com, and enter this book's unique code.

BOOK CODE

G692358

AV² by Weigl brings you media enhanced books that support active learning.

...and much, much more!

Published by AV² by Weigl
350 5th Avenue, 59th Floor New York, NY 10118
Websites: www.av2books.com   www.weigl.com

Copyright ©2016 AV² by Weigl
All rights reserved. No part of this publication may be reproduced, stored in a retrieval system, or transmitted in any form or by any means, electronic, mechanical, photocopying, recording, or otherwise, without the prior written permission of the publisher.

Library of Congress Cataloging-in-Publication Data

Carr, Aaron.
  Rat / Aaron Carr.
    pages cm. -- (I love my pet)
  ISBN 978-1-4896-3102-2 (hardcover : alk. paper) -- ISBN 978-1-4896-3103-9 (softcover : alk. paper) -- ISBN 978-1-4896-3104-6 (single-user ebk.) -- ISBN 978-1-4896-3105-3 (multi-user ebk.)
 1. Rats as pets--Juvenile literature. 2. Rats--Juvenile literature. I. Title.
  SF459.R3C374 2014
  636.935'2--dc23
                                         2014038595

Printed in the United States of America in North Mankato, Minnesota
1 2 3 4 5 6 7 8 9 0 18 17 16 15 14

112014
WEP311214

Project Coordinator: Katie Gillespie   Art Director: Terry Paulhus

Weigl acknowledges Getty Images and iStock as the primary image suppliers for this title.

I Love My Pet
RAT

CONTENTS

- 2   AV² Book Code
- 4   Rats
- 6   Life Cycle
- 10 Features
- 14 Care
- 20 Health
- 22 Rat Facts
- 24 Key Words
- 24 www.av2books.com

I love my pet rat.
I take good care of her.

5

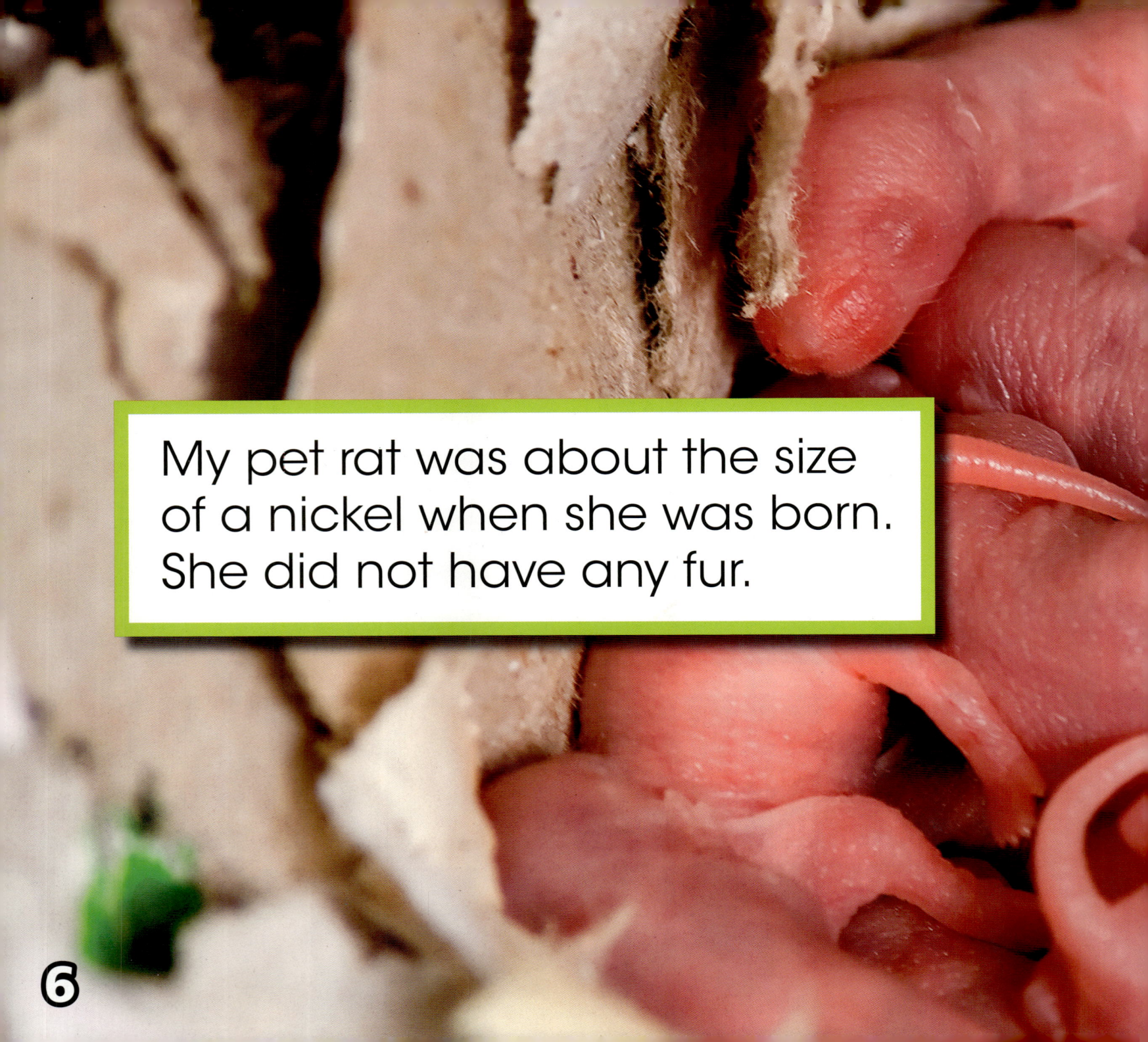

My pet rat was about the size of a nickel when she was born. She did not have any fur.

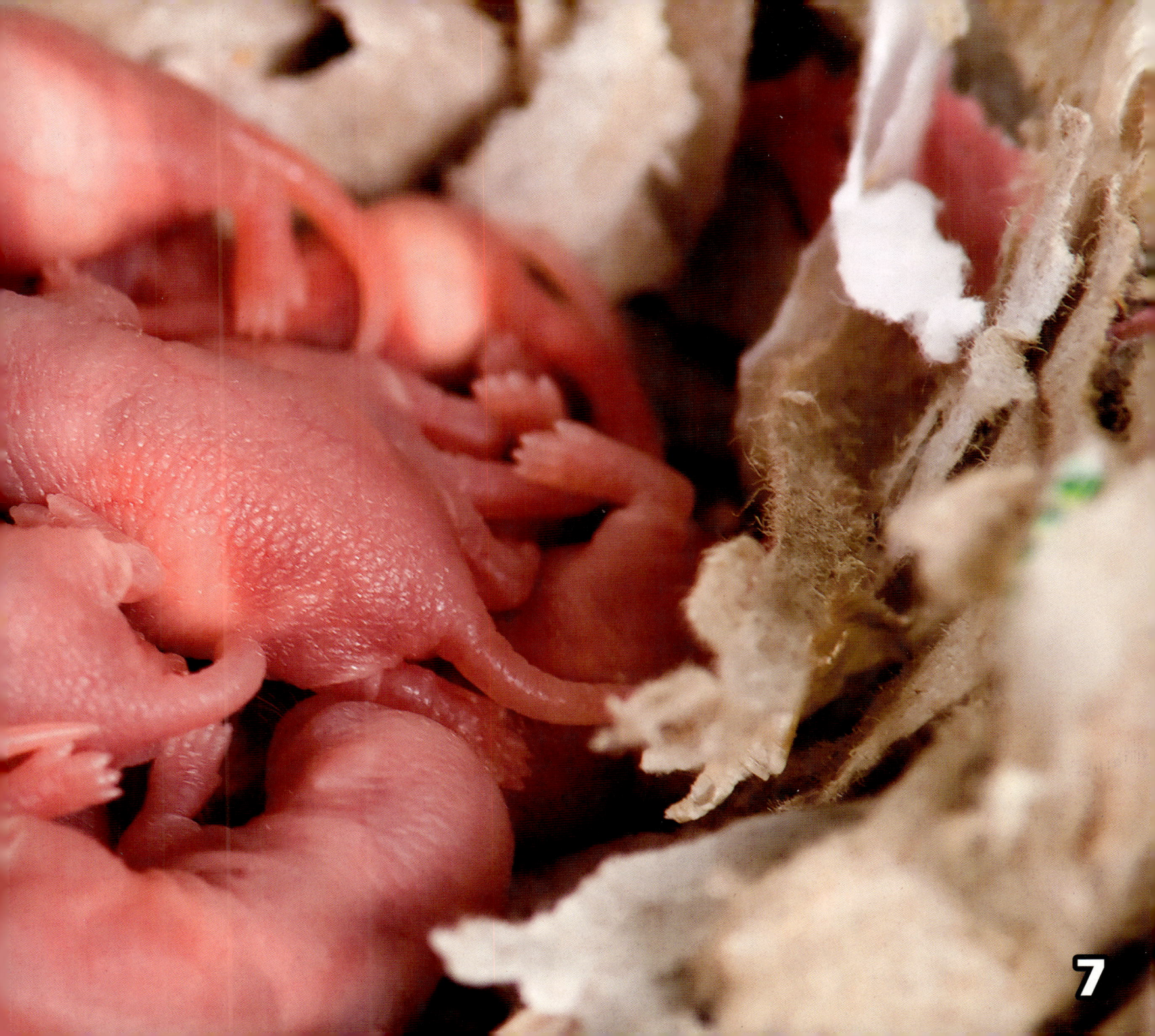

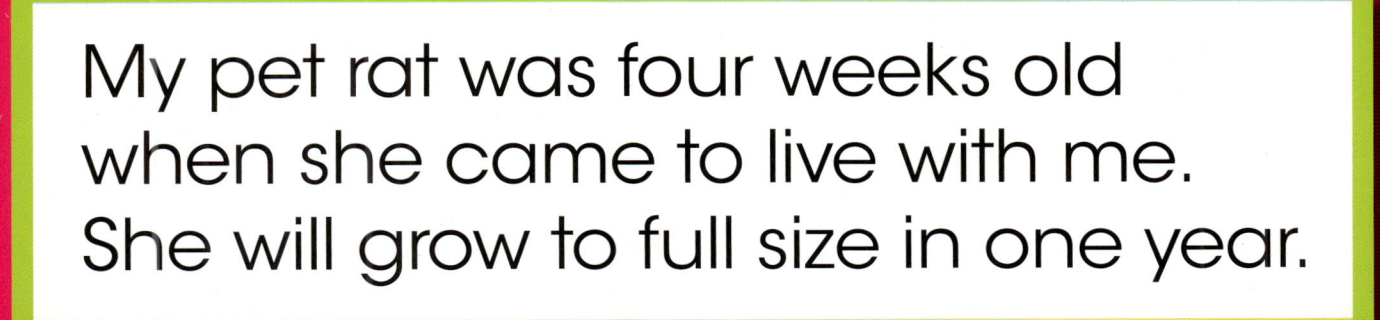

My pet rat was four weeks old when she came to live with me. She will grow to full size in one year.

Most rats live to be two or three years old.

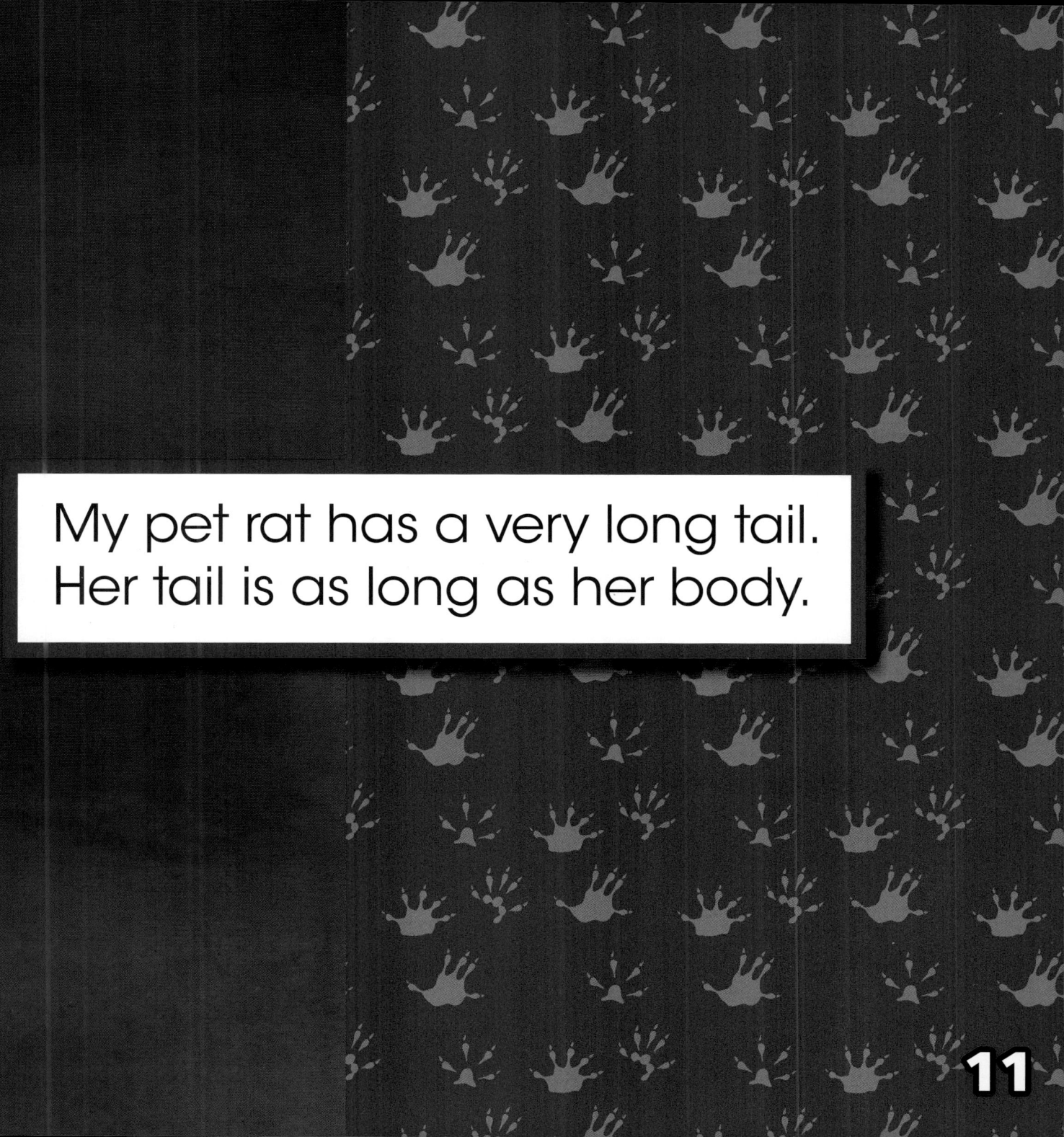

My pet rat has a very long tail. Her tail is as long as her body.

My pet rat has strong front teeth. These teeth never stop growing.

Rats also have flat teeth for chewing.

My pet rat needs food and water every day. I make sure she always has food in her dish.

My pet rat lives in a large cage.
I clean her cage when it gets dirty.

Rats need a warm and dark place to sleep.

My pet rat loves to play. I play with her every day to keep her happy.

I make sure my pet rat is healthy.
I love my pet rat.

RAT FACTS

These pages provide more detail about the interesting facts found in the book. They are intended to be used by adults as a learning support to help young readers round out their knowledge of each animal featured in the *I Love My Pet* series.

Pages 4–5

I love my pet rat. I take good care of her. Rats are part of the rodent family, which includes gerbils and squirrels. They are commonly kept as pets because they are small and quiet. Rats love to climb and play, and they are comfortable being handled by people. They can even be taught to do tricks.

Pages 6–7

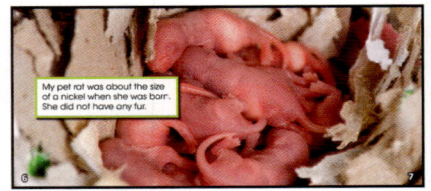

My pet rat was about the size of a nickel when she was born. She did not have any fur. Baby rats, or kittens, need their mother to protect and feed them. They only weigh about 0.2 ounces (7 grams) at birth. Kittens grow quickly. They begin to grow fur around one week old, and they open their eyes after about two weeks.

Pages 8–9

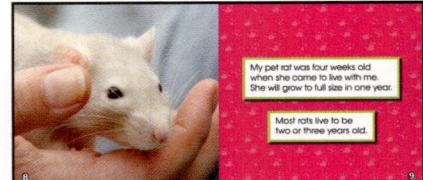

My pet rat was four weeks old when she came to live with me. She will grow to full size in one year. By three to four weeks, young rats are weaned and no longer depend on their mother. They are now ready to be taken to a new home. By this age, size differences between males and females become noticeable.

Pages 10–11

My pet rat has a very long tail. Her tail is as long as her body. Rats use their tails for balance and to help them find their way in the dark. Their tails also allow rats to maintain their body temperature. When they are warm, rats release heat by sending more blood into the tail, which cools quickly. When cold, rats conserve heat by sending less blood to the tail.

Pages 12–13

My pet rat has strong front teeth. These teeth never stop growing. Rats need to chew wood to keep their front teeth, or incisors, from growing too long. They use their incisors to break open hard shells and nuts. A rat's rear teeth, or molars, are used to chew food. They stop growing at a certain size.

Pages 14–15

My pet rat needs food and water every day. I make sure she always has food in her dish. Veterinarians recommend a diet of commercial rat pellets and fresh vegetables, such as broccoli or carrots. Rats can also eat fruit as an occasional treat. Pellets and clean water should always be available. Any uneaten fresh food should be removed after one day.

Pages 16–17

My pet rat lives in a large cage. I clean her cage when it gets dirty. Each pet rat needs about 2 cubic feet (0.06 cubic meters) of space. Wire cages with solid plastic or metal bottoms work best. The bottom of the cage should be lined with hay or litter pellets. Rats also need a nest, such as a small cardboard box with a hole cut in it.

Pages 18–19

My pet rat loves to play. I play with her every day to keep her happy. Rats are active animals. Once a rat is comfortable with its new home and owner, it can be held and petted. A happy rat may chatter or even lick its owner's fingers. Rats also grind their teeth together, or "brux," when they are happy.

Pages 20–21

I make sure my pet rat is healthy. I love my pet rat. A clean cage, a balanced diet, and regular play will keep most rats healthy. Rats kept in pairs or groups have fewer health issues than rats that live alone. They will play together, groom each other, and sleep in the same nest.

KEY WORDS

Research has shown that as much as 65 percent of all written material published in English is made up of 300 words. These 300 words cannot be taught using pictures or learned by sounding them out. They must be recognized by sight. This book contains 55 common sight words to help young readers improve their reading fluency and comprehension. This book also teaches young readers several important content words, such as proper nouns. These words are paired with pictures to aid in learning and improve understanding.

Page	Sight Words First Appearance
4	good, her, I, my, of, take
6	a, about, any, did, have, not, she, the, was, when
9	be, came, four, grow, in, live, me, most, old, one, or, three, to, two, will, with, year
11	as, has, is, long, very
12	also, for, never, stop, these
15	always, and, day, every, food, make, needs, water
16	gets, large, place
18	play

Page	Content Words First Appearance
4	care, pet, rat
6	fur, nickel, size
9	weeks
11	body, tail
12	teeth
15	dish
16	cage

Check out www.av2books.com for activities, videos, audio clips, and more!

1. Go to www.av2books.com.
2. Enter book code. G692358
3. Fuel your imagination online!

www.av2books.com